T0324401

TROPICALIA

THE ANDRÉS MONTOYA POETRY PRIZE

2004, *Pity the Drowned Horses*, Sheryl Luna
Final Judge: Robert Vasquez

2006, *The Outer Bands*, Gabriel Gomez
Final Judge: Valerie Martínez

2008, *My Kill Adore Him*, Paul Martínez Pompa
Final Judge: Martín Espada

2010, *Tropicalia*, Emma Trelles
Final Judge: Silvia Curbelo

The Andrés Montoya Poetry Prize, named after the late California native and author of the award-winning book, *The Iceworker Sings*, supports the publication of a first book by a Latino or Latina poet. Awarded every other year, the prize is administered by Letras Latinas— the literary program of the Institute for Latino Studies at the University of Notre Dame.

TROPICALIA

EMMA TRELLES

University of Notre Dame Press

Notre Dame, Indiana

Copyright © 2011 Emma Trelles
Published by the University of Notre Dame Press
Notre Dame, Indiana 46556
www.undpress.nd.edu
All rights Reserved

Manufactured in the United States of America

Library of Congress Cataloging-in-Publication Data

Trelles, Emma.
  Tropicalia / Emma Trelles.
      p. cm. — (The Andr?s Montoya Poetry Prize ; 2010)
  ISBN-13: 978-0-268-04236-3 (pbk. : alk. paper)
  ISBN-10: 0-268-04236-5 (pbk. : alk. paper)
  I. Title.
  PS3620.R4449T76   2011
  811'.6—dc22
                                      2010049635

∞ *The paper in this book meets the guidelines for permanence
and durability of the Committee on Production Guidelines for
Book Longevity of the Council on Library Resources.*

For Emma Quintanilla and Juan Garcia

madre y tio

teachers and twins

Contents

Part I

Part II

Acknowledgments

Many thanks to the editors and staff of the following publications, where these poems first appeared, at times in earlier versions:

3 AM Magazine: "Billy Bragg Rescues Us at the FTAA Protest"; "Churchill's Hideaway"; "Interstate Song"; "Love"; "Miami Postal Worker Shoots Two, Kills Self"

Gulf Stream Magazine: "Hunger"

MiPOesias: "In an Alcove Between the Beacon and the Avalon"; "Autumn, Unexpected"

New Millennium Writings: "From the Shorecrest, Miami Beach"

OCHO: "*Gua-Gua*"; "How to Write a Poem: Theory #62"; "If This Were a Restaurant Review"; "Novena Poderosa"; "What Would Have Happened If I Had Married You"

Poets and Artists: "Autorretrato Quintina"; "For the Woman on the Boulevard"; "Against the Blurring World"; "Election Abecedarian"; "The First Cold Night"

The Best American Poetry blog: "Lorca Is Green"

The Tigertail Poetry Annual: "Aubade"; "Chicken Lady"

Verse Daily: "Millificent"

Several poems here also appeared in the chapbook *Little Spells* (GOSS183 Press, 2008).

My deepest gratitude to the following for their care, guidance, and inspiration: Edward Trelles, Francisco Aragón, Silvia

Curbelo, Andrés Montoya, Letras Latinas, all at the University of Notre Dame Press, Christiaan Lopez-Miro, Campbell Mc-Grath, Didi Menendez and GOSS183, Denise Duhamel, Richard Blanco, Stacey Harwood, David Lehman, the BAP bloggers, The Guild Literary Complex, the Florida Center for the Literary Arts, Books and Books, the Miami Book Fair International, and my husband Mark Zolezzi, partner in life and art.

Introduction to the Poems

Tropicalia is, first and foremost, an atmosphere. Walking into these poems, one enters a soundscape where something akin to a heavy bass line underscores the scenery. Scraps of music and conversation mingle with the narration, and the rest is echo, feedback. Visually, the effect is pure motion, a long camera sweep of overpasses and street signs, tract houses, palm trees, gardens, weeds—all blown through with a language as insistent as a hot summer breeze.

When the dust settles on these pages, we find ourselves inhabiting a dialogue, a confession, a rant. What Emma Trelles offers us is a bridge to the other side of the argument, and a keen, almost mystical interaction with her surroundings that ultimately questions more than it reveals:

> Because the land is covered in salt.
> Because the land will not cede.
> Because I am rejected.
> Because I am released.

* * *

Tropicalia borrows its title from the Brazilian art movement of the same name, a vibrant blend of genres and styles that colored the international arts scene in the late '60s and early '70s. Edgier and more savvy than the flower-power hippie culture of its neighbors to the north, its vast creative energy drew from many different sources to shape a new hybrid most strongly felt in music, but also visual and performance art, poetry, film, and fashion.

As mirror, *Tropicalia* the book brings a similar energy to the mix. Trelles imbues her odd brew of poetic styles and voices with a strong visual sense. The result is a narrative infused with a powerful physicality of place. In keeping with the cinematic spirit of the poems, roads tangle and split, blacktop sizzles. Expressways crisscross the city and interstates cut the rain-soaked, verdant land in two. Color is provocation, and Trelles's own rustic palette provides the perfect hues. This is part and parcel of gritty, urban South Florida, where love ticks quietly in the shadows while the rest of the story is pure movieland circus, a place where Santa Barbara holds court with beer-drenched tourists and mystics and the future is a bus ride to anywhere (". . . the autopsy glow of the No. 9 / speeding through the beautiful shadows / made by caged windows and weeds").

In this nick-of-time road trip, the squeal and hum of the tires is as universal as prayer, voices raised to a ramshackle religion where the disenfranchised "pray for clarity, pray for vengeance," but also "where the sky at dusk is an altar / Chagall would have painted with his plain-faced angels."

Born from the clarity and distance of the involved observer, Trelles's slice of under-the-wire salvation is both the joy and genius in these poems. Beneath the "concrete and salt" of urban collapse and suburban sprawl, gardenias swell, the air around us is a chorus, the heart strains, the land takes us in. When the momentum finally slows, the hard edges have softened into something much more engaging and true.

—Silvia Curbelo,
Judge

Be not afeard; the isle is full of noises,
Sounds and sweet airs, that give delight and hurt not.
Sometimes a thousand twangling instruments
Will hum about mine ears; and sometimes voices . . .

—*The Tempest*

PART I

Some of the Reasons

Because there is a window.
Because there is rain.
Because the sky is a vault that houses the past.
Because there is a child and a father.
Because there is ruin.
Because it is the hour of visions and failing blue.
Because my lies are also the truth.
Because I love the alleys' footnotes and the just bridges of the bay.
Because I love the gravel rooftops and sentinel antennas.
Because there is an orange stripe of dusk in the west.
Because young men circle their bikes and sell respite.
Because they sell the promise of the noose.
Because the band was nomadic and took my head along.
Because a guitar is a box of air.
Because I can sing.
Because he pedals when he sleeps.
Because he kneeled and because he asked.
Because the land is covered in salt.
Because the land will not cede.
Because I am rejected.
Because I am released.
Because pelicans have returned to fish the inlet.
Because the moon is quartered.
Because the airport rises from the dark in a castle of light.

Interstate Song

On the drive home, a glory of crimson
lilies in the weave beside the blacktop,
a tangle of sawgrass and tupelo I imagine
leads to kingdoms of forgiveness, if only I could
find the doorknob, swing a square open and walk into
amnesia rain, drops shaped like doves and Pan-boys
humming and combing their beards. Of course
there would be smears of winged glitter
flying between the flame and the wick, voices
pitched in the perfect key of carnival glass.
I want to know what burrows beneath the eye.
I want to write *sky pearls* and see those two words
beaded together, what the great poet saw
when he looked up and traced
a chain of white buckets, a fit of summer
clouds glazing light and light glazing
the gutter puddles. Everything looks better in a poem,
or worse, depending on how much of the day you were able
to hoard and how much you gave and gave, and you're running
out of time, from the past, you'll climb into a cannon,
goggles tight and ears braced for the azure boom into the future:
a still life and the absence of mirrors and blades,
a palace where the cakes are laced with berries and you
have arrived, face smooth and tongue without doubt.

From the Shorecrest, Miami Beach

for Lee Anderson

What else would we have done with ourselves?
You wrote your way out of central Florida
land of camshafts and juke-punch psalms
an otherness so thick it sealed
your mouth with alien dust.
Mine was a death by Cuban-good-girl rules:
Always wear lipstick
Worship the father
Keep the true tongue still.

Somehow we found our way
to these Cadillac days, fat and floating
along Penn Avenue, where eyeless cops
brush by on bikes and the homeless knot
the corners in rags; at early light stereos
shake oaks with bass lines big enough
to bust the chest and coma heads wide open.

Nights we squat on the stoop
drinking *cafetasos*, talking sex, cashless
wishes, Carver and the Coen brothers, and the parade
rolls by with queens and high-piled hair
first generation girls, black flares and volcanic lipstick
first generation boys strutting boots and cabochon eyes
and the Hasidics inside their dusty flapping suits
pupils unfocused, not wanting to see what has fallen on
this city in a wave of jeweled decay.

Listen, when I said underbelly
I meant more than the constellations
slipped between concrete and salt, more than
the breathing self or the skin of dreams, this
place this place where the sky at dusk is an altar
Chagall would have painted with his plain-faced angels.

Billy Bragg Rescues Us at the FTAA Protest

I thought he was Tina's friend
the way she skipped up to him,
her ponytail swinging behind her
like a shiny propeller, like she was
on her way to a lemonade stand
at a carnival instead of running
hard from tear gas and rubber bullets.

I thought he looked like a fisherman
or one of those drunks who live
on crappy boats in the Keys,
buy their beer by the case and in the can.

But when he called to us
he raised his magic hand,
his fret-stitching hand,
each fingertip buffed and set with opals
bright enough to block the blood
shine of people beaten to the ground
but not so bright we forgot
where we were.

He slipped us his room key,
and we joined the lucky,
already saved, now all of us penned
inside the penthouse of the Holiday Inn,
having a holiday with bad
bar food and highballs and the kind of laughter
you hear at funeral parlors.

The lights went out and Billy Bragg glowed.
Our shadows pieced around him.
I touched his cheek, closed my eyes for luck.

Novena Poderosa

Fill the glass; light the wick,
prick three drops upon a sheet.
Honor the dead with gardenias,
stuff throats with the scent of forgiveness.
Honor the living with seasoned timber,
there is reckoning found in patience and plank.
Eat twelve grapes on the eve of each year,
your mind will wield a silvered resilience.
String a satchel of thistle to slit ill intentions,
an orange beneath the bed to sweeten
the heart's dark pockets.
Pray for clarity, pray for vengeance,
pray to la Santa Barbara, who favors
red carnations, spools fire
from her lips, her copper swords.

Letter to the Right

I hope you never read my poems.
I do not care for the sweet wine you serve
warm from the pantry, or the email you sent
about a savior at the supermarket.
Here's some news: He is not blonde. He is not watching.
When I saw him, he wore glasses and a beard
shaped like a flame. When I heard him,
his voice was a glissando of raw guitars and sorrows.
America, I don't remember who you belong to.
Even when I've smiled and said *thanks*, I've really meant *shut up*.
It is time to practice your hospital voice.
Somewhere there are silkworms making, and their music is
    redemption.
Somewhere there is a man with a gun, always a gun.
Near my home, a fence painted with the names of the dead.
Do you hear them between prayers, yours and mine?
I imagine the dead are dreaming of September
with its fading light and useful errands,
the dead assembled in soft robes.
This is the hour when I wanted to sleep
but I thought I would write you instead.

Gua–Gua

Could be the cry of a dog
or a cartoon baby's mouth
open to a pink cave of tonsils,
the squiggle lines of an animator's pen
bursting from his bald head.

Guaaaaa-Guaaaaa
the blank drone you hear when
you dial out of the Casa Bella in Oaxaca
or the bleat of dusty buses charging
streets alongside wagons dragged by mares.
In Mexico, it's *boooos,*
the slurred song of a beer-heavy ghost,
or the love charm Frida sang that lured
men and monkeys from the tamarind trees.

In Miami, Cuba, it's *gua-gua,*
the "w" sound of water brushed into a dream,
the war between *why* and *wait.*
Gua-gua,
the clipped cry from an imperfect memory,
a wish to travel in reverse
to an island shaped like a boomerang.
You can fling it as far as 90 miles and still
feel its edge in your hands.

Miami Postal Worker Shoots Two, Kills Self

I'm braiding dust for the mantle
where the candles tumble
when the trucks groan over the street.
I'm praying for Jesus
who's pressing his wings
flat on his sleeve, along with U.S.
and his name, which means bless you in Spanish.

Poor Jesus
he must feel pretty low
dragging that gun around
all day at the bottom of his bag,
his fingers kissing metal and light
bills that know his last breath before he takes it.

Did his girl bleed him first? Force him to live
without, poison his dog, bed his brother,
smash the collection of Lladro
willed to him by his *mami*?
Did she grind it up beneath her pointy pumps,
sew each shard into his scalp?

I'd like a crown like that,
something that could shine and cut.

I'm done with the nothing
I've twined for two hours
as long as it takes
Jesus to empty his sack,
except for the gun he holds by an oak
where he kneels
when his song
floats over the street:
We are braiding
We are braiding
We are braiding this dust.

Florida Poem

After summer rains,
marble thumb snails and beetles
blot the window screens
with pearl and drone. Gardenias swell,
breathing is aquatic and travel
a long drawl from bed to world.
During drought,
the heat becomes a devil
girl with oven-red lips
who wants your brains puddled
in a brass-capped mason jar,
who wants the silver stripped
from your tongue, the evening pulse
between your legs, yes, she wants
everything from you.

Desire

She imagines the way
his white shirt will shimmer
how his watch will press a blind eye
against the seasons ahead.
She imagines how his nails wind
into thick spirals, how the tiniest of creatures
finds path to the jelly of his eyes.
At last there is the matter of his shoes
ash black, sharp-toed, gleaming
like axes or the way we burn
when nothing is left.

Churchill's Hideaway

Thursday and it's pure night-of-the-living
dead, garbage weeds and assorted moon men
weaving through dumpsters, eyes
sucked into sockets, hands balled, a need
to clamp down on something more solid
than the rusted hulks in the parking lot.

I can't resist this gravity anymore than Lot's
wife could avoid looking back, the living
host always on tap, a bought and sold
communion with down-and-out shrimpers, men
plucking butts from the gutter, regulars needing
the fix and the bands that blind our ears

to the intimate echo, the *I'm alone* chant
spinning skulls until the allotted night arrives.
Then we lean back on the patio, good weed
smoothing brows, the din of the living
around us, pool balls clacking, matches struck, men
betting on soccer and horses, pinballs belling. The solid

rhythm of neon hisses from windows long sealed
against light. Each week we look forward to iced
glass, Fenders and feedback meant
for hollowing heads. We salute, snub, lock
arms around waists, old parachutes leafing
the ceiling with angel-pale skins. We find needles

by the toilet and spoons cooked clean,
baggies empty of their drifting solace.
We love it here, and peel losses from our skins
like failed saints, our good eyes veiled
when we leave. Let us linger in this dusted lot
until the lights go out and the street men

nestle in shadow, ready for sleep and a day meant
for more than forgetting. I have often knitted
my own amnesia here, stood outside plotting
second chances and success, wondered if the oiled
likeness mantling the doorway really is Churchill, eyes
lizard-curious, teeth brown-ridged and biting.

Noise Band Concerto

Now each player takes his mark
on crooked planks and slabs of rug
in light gelled red and steadied on the wall.
Now each piece stroked and strung,
frets secured, cymbals skewered,
valves and sliders polished. Now each
switch flips rubber veins siphon
the almighty, holiest of holy, juice,
sizzle, power, preen. Now sound
breaks, painful stutter, scrape of tin
on glass, now expansion, accordionic
wah-wah pedals, distortion boxes,
samplers humming static and outer space
signals, now the shapely hip of a cotton-gagged
cello, now lascivious bass and tambourine shamble,
now the trumpet bellows discordant brass, herald
of gladiators, cerulean banners and forgotten women,
now percussion, high-hat hiss, beaded obsidian,
hammers working bone, the pulse felt at the hollow,
the fleshy eye, adrenaline tectonic, reverb of subterfuge,
now water pounding, canyon forging, quarried oceans
and the underground rivers of the heart, what swims there is
frantic for purchase, the way of gun barrels, the way of locks.

Aubade

After acid we spoon strawberry ice cream
straight from the tub. Finger our eyes. Make sure
we have not abandoned them to last night's
reel of violin blur, Parthenon acoustics,
crippled mystics trapped in Dali-wood.
Our skins have stopped their cellophane crackling.
Dawn pools her quiet tonic over us
eating this cold sweetness, legs coiled,
chemical mouths stitched together.
Even the birds have not uttered their spells
at this hour of sanctity and small victories.

What Would Have Happened
If I Had Married You

We buy a house. Not one of those Spanish-tiled numbers that have drowned this town with their stealthy shine; our home has hardwood dignity, pewter fixtures, fruit trees out back. We hire a cleaning lady. Her name is Pilar. She dusts the grain and amber furniture, cooks our dinner at night—*gallo pinto*, plantains, all forms of slaughtered meat. Pilar smokes on the back patio. She makes me want to smoke too, only I can't because I'm trying to get pregnant and read that I should purge myself of all I love before conceiving. At night I listen for your snore, wait for your octopus stretch across the bed. I slip across the patio, past key lime, mango, sapodilla and mamey. White-soled and ravenous, I climb branches, swallow skins, save the seeds for later, knowing even the shriveled ones can bear life.

Country Dada Song, in 4/4 Time

The devil's in my rearview mirror
and he's larger than he appears.
He's smiling at me with his bottlecap teeth
and his eyes are filled with beer.
I don't know how he got here
but I wish he'd go away,
down the hole of a donkey's anus
or may-be to Maa-drid, Spain.

The devil's in my rearview mirror
and he's closer than he appears.
His fingers click like needles.
He's licking up my tears.
I don't know why he clocks me;
I just wish he'd disappear,
like a wily sock at the Laundromat
or a tick in my cat's ear.

Waterfall banjo
Waterfall banjo
Waterfall banjo

I often wonder why
I live my life in such despair,
why Satan's always after me—
He's almost everywhere.

It doesn't matter if I've stumbled
or I've played it straight;
that Bag of Ash won't stop until
I'm heaped upon his plate.

Reporter's Notebook

January afternoon. Cold and bright. Should be more industrious, amass further facts for this month's cover story: visitor attendance (300,000), membership (35,000), acreage (83), and subdivisions (9) of Fairchild Tropical Botanic Garden. Dullness! Better to sit here on this little bench near the lake and delight: iguanas gold and green, happy creak of bamboo, buff-bellied hummingbird floating over swamp bush. Silk heads of sabal palms. A fine place to picnic. Should bring Mark and hummus sandwiches. Strawberries too. Are they in season? Yesterday renowned glass artist said he's pleased to return to the garden with his elysian confections: liquid blazed, blown and tooled into petals and spires, into ropy towers reflected in ponds. I ask how and why. He tells me the acreage is nice. Fact: no amount of drilling can make a person say something interesting. My deadline stalks me. Doom. Soon I must file my story and pray the copy desk doesn't mangle my verbs or use quotation marks "for emphasis." Fact: cycads are the oldest seed plants on earth and predate the dinosaurs (check this). Fact: the iguanas have now vanished along with the sun. Lake fills with dusk. Glass spheres float and twirl across water, color of sherbert, mint, impossible gloss—delicate as bubbles blown from a child's toy loop. This will be my opening graf. Thank you capricious gods! Thank you silver-leaf oaks and fading sky. Ballad for flora and twilight. Reminds me of that Tennyson poem. Is there a way to work it into the story? *Now sleeps the crimson petal, now the white . . . now lies the Earth all Danaë to the stars.* What comes in between these lines? Something else I don't remember.

Chicken Lady

Gunshots, back alley screams, cats
caught in garbage bins and the rubber-faced man
who paced my front sidewalk day and night,
his back spooled to a lowercase *r*.
At dawn I plotted murder when the santera
next door sang rum and holy cadence
to her nicotine chickens.

You pay a price for spackle and spit,
for rent, Raid, utilities. Then the drop-kick
fee no one tells you about for living
in the guts of your city.
It can pick your skull clean.

I moved to a land of green
medians and swept gutters,
guillotine windows and invisible neighbors.
The cats are collared, the garbage doubles as sculpture.
I am five minutes from arterial highways,
holistic parks, the best and brightest pre-k's. I'm cornered
by oak, ficus, streets named *Pleasantberry* and *Sweetlover*.

I've bought a chick, the puffed and peeping kind.
We watch for sirens and salesmen, eat pears and pecan pie.
At night, stars shine like knives through my eyelids.
There are snakes in the trees.
I can hear the ticking of their tongues.

Hunger

A rusty crab picks across the gold-packed sand—
first time in years I see anything
besides napkins and foil working the shore.
Must be that hole in the ozone, knitting itself together,
a surge of redemption, nudging all matters into light.
Never mind they're hiding
boats off the coast of Cojimar, patched rafts and blind
wooden boxes sagging against the sea, mothers
with dead hands, boys broken with thirst,
the same way my grandfather looked the day he flew
    in from Havana,
skin the color of dry clay and corneas glazed like porcelain.
No food, he said, there's nothing left.
They're trapping cats in the fields.
They fill you up all right; just shut your eyes and eat.

If This Were a Restaurant Review

I'd start in scene, something about marble and salt and the coil
of curls crowning the waitress, the tide of cheese fries and
    burgers
heading to the terrace of the Tudor Hotel, to our table, near a
    tourist-flecked ocean,
a winter's length away from asphalt light, trains, the pie-slab of
    five boroughs

still dusted with snow even in March; New York City—
where once my tie-dyed ass posed in front of Trump Tower
for a photo I ruined by flipping a stiff middle finger at the glass
    and brass
doors. On this same trip, I dropped a penny from the top of the
    true

Towers, now unmade, but then still poking their own heads into
    the clouds,
high above a city of glazed pedestrians who might take my
    copper offer
straight to the nose, the flaky scalp, or at least through the toe
    of a well-buffed shoe.
Afterwards, I sat at the Kiev and ate a cold bowl of blood. It
    was good.

Here on Miami Beach, tricked out choppers rain chrome on
    Collins Ave.,
taxis and tattoo needles click in 4/4 time. It's the kind of beat
    you can rely on.
If this were a restaurant review, I would use the words *retro* and
    mustard,
leave out how the red velvet jazz blowing through the stereo

reminds me of Robert De Niro in *Taxi Driver*, not the part
    where he's burning
the tendons in his forearm over a gas stove, or when he takes
    his date to a porn palace,
but the ending, when he drives off in his checkered chariot,
    streets slick with rain, traffic
lights washing each city block in garnet, green, the plain
    promise of yellow.

PART II

How to Write a Poem: Theory #62

The beginning should eat the eyes.
It's the part of the movie where you step into line
at the bodega with Our Lady of the Sponge Curlers.
She's buying toilet paper and Mahatma rice. This is her life
and you happened to ease into it at the wooden lull
between explosions.

You could also begin while she's watching
her husband drop the scotch he's sucked for days,
hear glass break magnificent rain over the linoleum.

If you are still mouthless
use *seraphim* and *penumbra*.
Both will drape the frame in velvet,
pearl the hems with high art and smart girl words that hide
god please god don't let me flinch fail fall into the dark.
A mention of Babel or blackberries
wouldn't hurt either.

The question of where to snap
the line at its finest edge
can freeze the brain with dread.
The blade must be sharp enough to halve
the moon and the dark
clutter of sky.
Ignore this for
the moment.

There is nothing left
except the flutter of wings beneath the stabbing,
a woman before the stove, stirring rice and wishing death,
the river outside her window, how it glosses after rain
not like mirrors or a polished lens, simply
water, falling, dark.

Autorretrato Quintina

A mind needs a place to set its teeth, and grace
arrives in fixing the toilet, in water
smoothing the pre-dawn fears of possible
cysts, faulty seatbelts, the radio loop
of reasons I'm needed and belong nowhere.

Here is a mirror without *Las Meninas*, and nowhere
does light soften brow and wrist to the grays
blessed by Velázquez. Here is a needle's loop
for a mouth. Here is a sheet of water
rising behind the iris, here, the possible

a mottled gold. My skin is a plausible
way of counting miles, the tender nowhere
route of veins, tongue floating in water
carried since birth. My hands have the grace
to wield a wrench, to pull a chain loop

free from its knots and sketch the oval loop
a portrait might make if the impossible
appeared: a king's room brushed with grace,
sun fixed to lace and a leisure nowhere
near the bathroom echo of iron and water.

In this lull between doing and dreaming, water
owns shadow and animal rust, water loops
music around the heads of all who are nowhere
in the path of sleep. Draw closer. It is possible
to love the trouble in this face, to surrender.

For the Woman on the Boulevard

You're not really crying
because your car spit Hephaestus
smoke into the night and is now
sagging by the gutter, are you?
Feeling alone and poisoned
by vermouth and too much
tobacco rolled with the last
bit of spit and a one-dollar bill?
Can't deny the veins bracing
your temples and the pending
nightmares of the face, the inexorable
atlas you have read every hour you have
worried every dead and breathing skin?
Did you just once over the tow man?
Drink his thick wrists, his hands
shifting, turning the wheel, calling
the radio with his bossanova tongue
this master crafter of all you can't—
the call, the fix, the winch?
Did you part your knees for him
behind the garage before he took off
to rescue the next? Did he cover your mouth
when you cried—did you like it?

Are you riding the city bus, consoling
yourself in the autopsy glow of the No. 9
speeding through the beautiful shadows
made by caged windows and weeds
in fountains along the alleys? Are you
comforted by your invisibility? Does it
float you far above the day's shame?
Is it your only weapon? Do you hear it?
The whale hum of elevator carrying
you home, soft television, water
pouring dishes, tub, and teapot,
do you hear the needle spinning
once more to the horizon, slowly
clicking minutes towards the one
true star? Are you inside it
now, your bed, quilts stroking
the body's line, the moon
rise of head and hips
sketched in lamplight, seen
from perfect lawns
below, where a fox pads
a pale line to the inlet,
the bridge, to the room
where you dream.

Love

I keep asking if he'll try and find me
after we leave this world, in the next place,
whatever shining white nothing that entails.
I ask him most after watching apocalyptic
movies where the palette is nothing
but metals and dirt, and the weak are caged,
the hero without hope but with courage
and no one laughs, especially not the children
left to endure because that is what children do.
Will you try and meet me, even if
our shapes are smudged beyond recognition?
He tells me he doesn't know, doesn't know
what is next, pretending not to see the virgin
statues we've collected, crosses, candles lit
for scent and gratitude, but mostly to ward off
what could come along and cut us apart.
I say nothing else. I don't know how to explain
what I really mean, although *do not leave me*
is close, and what would the next long jaunt be
without the smell of him tracing the sheets,
without his hands?

Nocturne in Parts

postcard from Lethe

A trip to Virginia the psychic is like visiting
a *tia abuela*'s house: white tile, Boltaflex, kitchen
smells of *mojo* and Formica table sponged and damp.
You see this? She holds my hand between her scissor
fingers and tells me I should have died at 25.
When she's done, I walk to the park and watch
a pigeon slap his wings hard against the wind.
All that strain and he only makes it to the curb.
I barely made it out of bed this morning.
The kitchen fairies hid the oatmeal.
I settled for an orange.
There is something all-powerful and holy
about a cold orange. Imagine peeling
each day into one flawless strip.

the news

Maybe he just wanted some downtime,
his mind tired from clacking like an old Super 8,
clicking off real and imagined reels
the way we do when it's late and the house is unlit
and the air conditioner is the only breathing we can hear.
Maybe the silence he walked into was a relief.

not how it looks

Summer vines and bottlebrush,
ground fed with rain and sneaker tread.
Citronella flames smudge the lines.
I am a new geometry.
I am the queen of feathered masks.

odometer

Walking to the corner store for chocolate and incense
among strangers dreaming their own errands.
What happens after death?
I hope the next place is not too lonely.

required reading

Lime and salt avocado halves.
Light votives.
Bathe. Sleep.

storage

My mother's wedding portrait.
My father's handkerchief, still squared and pressed.
Letters from Pedrito in his just-in-case English:
At night I dream with all of us
together, table set, gardenias and wine
my sisters in white dresses
the front door unlocked.

portrait miniature

Today I saw a baby toad in the cherry hedge.
It was enough.

The Living Hour

Caped in sage and chalk-moon brooch

the sky arrives. The offering is wet

grass, a whipstitch of bird song.

How does its nickel pitch thread

April's blue quartz light?

How does it find hold in the whorl of the ear?

It is not enough to paint a place.

Let me offer my confession, then

amidst my unseen neighbors, the sly

tarpon cutting tunnels beneath

the inlet, the wild blood of branches.

I am a woman of doubt. I am a woman

running from my youth. I might rest a while

in this little kingdom, not map escape but

                                    fall

backwards   liquid   floating

down to where plain thoughts await.

It is the dream of all worriers, to silence

the dirge that has trailed us since birth.

Look here: desk   window

the city diminished

rolled back its carpet of gears and wailing.

This Week

I don't want to forget the walks
after day dissolved the parkway,
how air is an animal draped over skin
in July. We tracked egrets sailing
white over us, in pairs, a half hundred,
until we found them origami-folded
in the needles of slash pines.
Is it like this for everyone? Each nicking
minute, the ritual laments, then without
herald, the familiar, carrying you to clean
fields once more, thankful to be standing
in the heat watching egrets.

Against the Blurring World

Fat black teapot on a mahogany table;
fresh bread and pebbled streets;
early light illuminating fronds,
each leaf a body of veins, delicate and red;
moisture lifting earth in clouds of wet smoke;
grass jeweled with dew and milk gnats;
an upside-down scarab bicycling legs at the sky;
the ocean the ocean the ocean the ocean;
outdoor market a clutter of limes and pears,
pomegranates splitting skins, kerchiefed women
stringing mackerel; the tinny barks of dogs
on street corners as an orange kitten smacks his breakfast
beside a tub of wildflowers, where a street performer pulls
doves and coins from children's ears.

Autumn, Unexpected

The problem with buying concert tickets in advance:
you never know what axis you'll be resting on
when the not-so-grand event arrives; say it's Jane's Addiction,
sewn-up and slap-lacquered just in time to join the musty
clans of reunion tours, looping the country like shriveled
troubadours, in search of hands to make them whole.
At least the nights have lost their heated metal edge
and the moon is ringed in amethyst and slate
and the band has somehow crept through
a city of bodies to a small off-stage altar.
Kites spin above heads. Dust rises and takes flight.

In an Alcove Between the Beacon and the Avalon

Hotels, sure, but also pastel monoliths to fortune and revival,
to traveler's palms, to citronella, to mambo and techno;
Praise bay leaves, star jasmine, alleyways
seeded with saffron and ordered refuse,
praise the diamond-clad ships cruising the horizon,
fluid and pre-ordained, and the sky
chalked cobalt and plum, everything
rose-soaked until the very air is watercolored solace.

So what if we're rum-drunk, if we dined on too much
chocolate and salt and the good meat of grouper?
These are the godly nights, belonging exactly
to what is loved: a friend's voice, the familiar
hands at the elbow, and the wind plying
the skin with autumn, showing how
beauty is better felt than seen, how
gratitude is another word for joy.

What Escopazzo Means

for Mark

Here, it's crazy, my love explains,
but not really quite that, and he looks just as delicious
in his Adidas as the fresh black truffle, the risotto,
the cumulus of asparagus flan. I picture fields
ridged with fat stalks and a flourish of leaves,
acres framed by coral gates, a cottage, a rose bed,
two cats curled in shade and the front door swung open.

Parmigiano, he says, *grazie,* and our crystal chimes C# when we
    toast.
I know I'm wanted. We talk of glass and gardens, how Tennyson
    wished
for a love that silenced cypress trees and meteors. *Wait, you have to
    do this first,*
and he paints a plate with olive oil, coarse pepper and salt. We sit
    among the bribes
offered us, linen, silver, a candelabra with bulbs shaped like rain or
    the lights we looped
across the balcony one night, so late the moon had set and even the
    crickets hushed.

White, red, the licorice bite of the last swallow. A pairing,
the chef calls it, how food is chemistry or a harmony for the tongue.
If you order the wrong wine, you won't taste the heart flavors.
I know it's too rich, *il vino de pasto,* the blur of courses,
the final sweetness of lime crème brûlée and cantaloupe soup;
I know it's too much, the love-ness of this poem, but I am deep in it,
waist high in a swell of vineyards and lakes
brimming with blue, blue sky.

Heading into the Everglades

On a highway that threads through the cypress
I have seen an almost African land,
a green and patient form of stillness.

The road rivers through two horizons,
palmetto and dragonflies flower the ground
by the highway that threads through the cypress.

Gravel spits from backs of trucks
and colonies of ibis plant their knobbed
legs in the still grasses, part their patient beaks.

Then the hand-painted signs and sideshows,
Gas-N-Crafts, *Swamp Safari*, *Gators Live and Fed*.
All honor the highway that threads through the cypress.

Then the dread melaleuca, the dirt roads
leading to unmarked houses, smoke curling from solid
roofs, and women cooking with sweet grass and patience.

Once I saw a woman carrying lilies
out of the marshes that shadow the land
out of a green and patient stillness
beside the highway that threads through the cypress.

Millificent

No one has entered
the stone of this place
in a century, the dust has powdered
even the cat's lashes. Still I sit, robes folded, crown
pinned upon the river of my braids, their diamond
points have not forgotten how to find the door.
Once there were feasts here, tables set in silk, glazed peacock
and pomegranates so ripe a look from me would tear their skins.

I love the quiet.
The void of voices begging me
for youth and vengeance, for the fastest way
to travel over water or how to spy by moonlight.
I love how my hands do little but settle on my velvet lap.

Afternoons I rise to circle the gardens, the devil's trumpet large
enough now to shade all that lies beneath: moss, pond, the small
star blossoms that burst in clumps along the earth, so bright,
content to bleed their red selves into shadow.

The First Cold Night

What is this pool of silver, good
witch mirror, pearl plucked
from the neck of the world?

Eye pining for its own
reflection, opal shadow, a magic
lamp waiting for the rub.

Here is the darkest flame,
oval pulse, sword in mouth light,
flint, foil, head and hoof light, tail

lights, a red row stacked along the avenue,
brake lights bracketing the names of planets and wars
dimmed by time: Saturn, Mercury, Coupe de Ville.

I could loop this island twice on my bike
without pedaling, I could finish the unfinished,
deconstruct the ditties of parking lot finches, I could

straddle the man I have already met,
kiss his skin, Neruda him
with *tus ojos oceánicos*, and we'd rise
above the bed, bodies pale and sheltered
by a dome of stars forever lit.

I'm not kidding.
This night with its illicit coolness
can make you believe
anything.

Election Abecedarian

The duende's arrival always means a radical change in forms.
It brings to old planes unknown feelings of freshness, with the
quality of something newly created, like a miracle, and it produces
an almost religious enthusiasm.

—*Federico García Lorca*

A homemade soup was the best ticket I could think of,
    a tin pot paean to split pea,
Bliss potatoes and jasmine rice, an attainable target for a
    beginner who holds
Calm and remembers to make each task as important as the
    next. I am not that smooth,
Doomed instead to wash two cups of green pebbles and forget
    to vanquish the ones

Embossed with Lilliputian dents or bent with haste.
    Everything goes into the broth,
Flawed and whole, stirring, tracking the television maps red as
    autumn apples or like blue
Gulfs washing salt across shores. This is where I'm stalled.
    This is where I find it
Hard to say how those four hours and 53 minutes spiraled
    around us in a silver lasso

Inlaid with thorns. The room contracted and sound parceled
    verse: stove ticking couplets,
Jets dragging light through night clouds. When I was a girl
    I feared the future and its eyes
Kinked at the pupils so I could never tell if it was plotting
    dullness or ambush, or looking

Left, ignoring me for the granite stretch of years ahead.
	This is where courage lies in

Making peas boil to cream, knowing flame will mollify the
	hardest of the lot.
No, this is not metaphor, or a sly index of the unstoppable
	turning. We wanted to eat.
Or perhaps ready our mouths and bellies for whatever arrived,
	mind or sword, the best
Prayers chanted between bites. O' god of lucky numbers and
	linen closet altars, saint of all

Quiet words drilled into the dark, before breath slows its beat
	and body fades to sleep. Did you
Reel from the voices, nicked and mellifluous, or were our
	pleas as ordinary as the next minute?
Say the bread was hot and our bowls were filled. Say we
	danced and kissed into the long hours,
Toasted with bad champagne unearthed from the fridge.
	It was as destined as the alphabet,

Undulating, yet sure-footed in the march from shape to shape,
	the dive and rise of U,
V shaking lake from wing, and finches followed, trailing fire
	over backyards and alleys,
W gray and shorn, criminal arms flung upwards in surrender
	and not one wince of regret.
X at least held its center for the evening, and all the way
	through January, and after that

You could only bite down and wait. But those first months
	were crisp, limned with green
Zeal, and soil tilled and watered and humming with light.

Lorca Is Green

Federico García Lorca was a poet with deep-set eyes and a hood of thick eyebrows. When pressed together, his lips resembled two curved shells. He was a diminutive man who walked with a limp. His hands were delicate and resembled a child's.

I see Lorca, his words but also his body, what must now only be his disassembled bones, his prettiness and his flaws dissolved to minerals. He is perhaps buried near Granada, where hundreds of men and women were executed by gunshot in 1936, during the Civil War, beside a cemetery wall and its surrounding hillsides and olive trees.

Lorca died in summer, four months before the olive harvest, when the trees' silvered branches were likely heavy with petals and fruit. Some of them are very old, their leaves long threaded by a wind arriving from the sea, through a vacant archway, as Lorca wrote, *con olor de saliva de niño, de hierba machacada y velo de medusa.* It is a wind that attends the living.

Lorca is green as the sky at the hour of the *crepúsculo*, when the moon begins its bright ascent and the sidewalks fall to darkness. Lorca is the shadow-green of mangroves and pines, the slash of green beneath the egret's eye. He is the green that enters in silence; he is the green that returns.

Lorca was a poet whose work I read out loud and in Spanish to my mother and stepfather. She made Cuban coffee and served it in tiny china cups. He sat at the kitchen counter and noted, kindly, that my pronunciation was better than he had expected, quite good, in fact.

That summer when my mother's hair had finally grown back after the chemo, her head now dark and budding with curls, I could read *espadas* and *adelfa* but did not know they meant *swords* and *oleander*. It is easier to speak than to understand, Spanish, with its velvet-clad consonants and hopeful vowels, each letter sounding exactly as it appears. Nothing is left behind. Nothing is buried.

When my mother says my name, her voice rings like a little gold bell, and I think of yellow, a color that, like her, is filled with resolve. Yellow is a window, a locket, a poison that can heal. Yellow is Pinar del Rio—heat and flat valleys and where my mother's people are from. When I was a girl, yellow was the braid she wore long and down the middle of her back; yellow was the garden of succulents she grew, their branches circuitous and each leaf's shape a surprise: a paddle, a button, a dagger, a heart.

Notes

Billy Bragg is an English-born musician and political activist who fuses folk and punk rock in his songs. In November 2003, he kept several people from harm during a protest in Miami against the Free Trade Area of the Americas.

Gua-gua is the Cuban-Spanish word for "bus."

The title of "Miami Postal Worker Shoots Two, Kills Self" was taken from a UPI newspaper headline.

In "Interstate Song," "a chain of white buckets" is from "End of Summer" by W. S. Merwin.

"Against the Blurring World" is a phrase borrowed from Robert Hass's "Natural Theology."

In "The First Cold Night," "*tus ojos oceánicos*" is from "*Inclinado En Las Tardes*" / "Leaning into the Afternoons," a poem by Pablo Neruda.

"*con olor de saliva de niño, de hierba machacada y velo de medusa*" was found in "*Juego y teoría del duende*" (Play and Theory of the Duende), a lecture first given in Buenos Aires in 1933 by Federico García Lorca.

ABOUT THE AUTHOR

Emma Trelles received her Master of Fine Arts in Creative Writing from Florida International University. She is the winner of the 2010 Andrés Montoya Poetry Prize, the recipient of a Green Eyeshade Award for art criticism, and a regular contributor to the *Best American Poetry* blog. She is the author of the chapbook *Little Spells*, a recommended read by the *Valparaiso Poetry Review* and the *Montserrat Review*. She lives with her husband in South Florida, where she teaches and writes about visual art, books, and culture.

CPSIA information can be obtained
at www.ICGtesting.com
Printed in the USA
LVHW031545111221
705947LV00005B/178

9 780268 042363